MW01477509

little backyard animals

Deer

Samantha Nugent

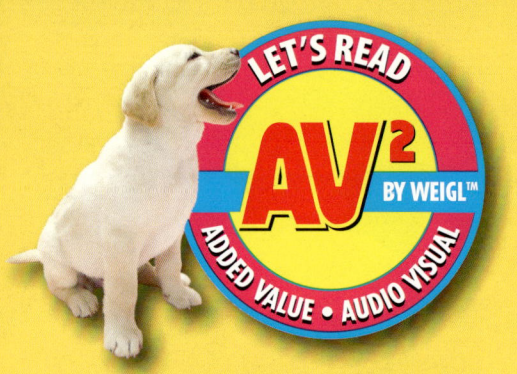

LET'S READ AV² BY WEIGL
ADDED VALUE • AUDIO VISUAL

AV² provides enriched content that supplements and complements this book. Weigl's AV² books strive to create inspired learning and engage young minds in a total learning experience.

Your AV² Media Enhanced books come alive with...

Audio
Listen to sections of the book read aloud.

Video
Watch informative video clips.

Embedded Weblinks
Gain additional information for research.

Try This!
Complete activities and hands-on experiments.

Key Words
Study vocabulary, and complete a matching word activity.

Quizzes
Test your knowledge.

Slide Show
View images and captions, and prepare a presentation.

... and much, much more!

Go to www.av2books.com, and enter this book's unique code.

BOOK CODE

P682462

AV² by Weigl brings you media enhanced books that support active learning.

Published by AV² by Weigl
350 5th Avenue, 59th Floor New York, NY 10118
Website: www.av2books.com

Copyright ©2017 AV² by Weigl
All rights reserved. No part of this publication may be reproduced, stored in a retrieval system, or transmitted in any form or by any means, electronic, mechanical, photocopying, recording, or otherwise, without the prior written permission of Weigl Publishers Inc.

Library of Congress Control Number: 2015958825

ISBN 978-1-4896-4747-4 (hardcover)
ISBN 978-1-4896-4810-5 (softcover)
ISBN 978-1-4896-4748-1 (multi-user eBook)

Printed in the United States of America in Brainerd, Minnesota
1 2 3 4 5 6 7 8 9 0 19 18 17 16 15

122015
041215

Project Coordinator: Heather Kissock
Designer: Terry Paulhus

Every reasonable effort has been made to trace ownership and to obtain permission to reprint copyright material. The publisher would be pleased to have any errors or omissions brought to its attention so that they may be corrected in subsequent printings.

The publisher acknowledges Corbis Images, Getty Images, Alamy, and iStock as the primary image suppliers for this title.

Deer

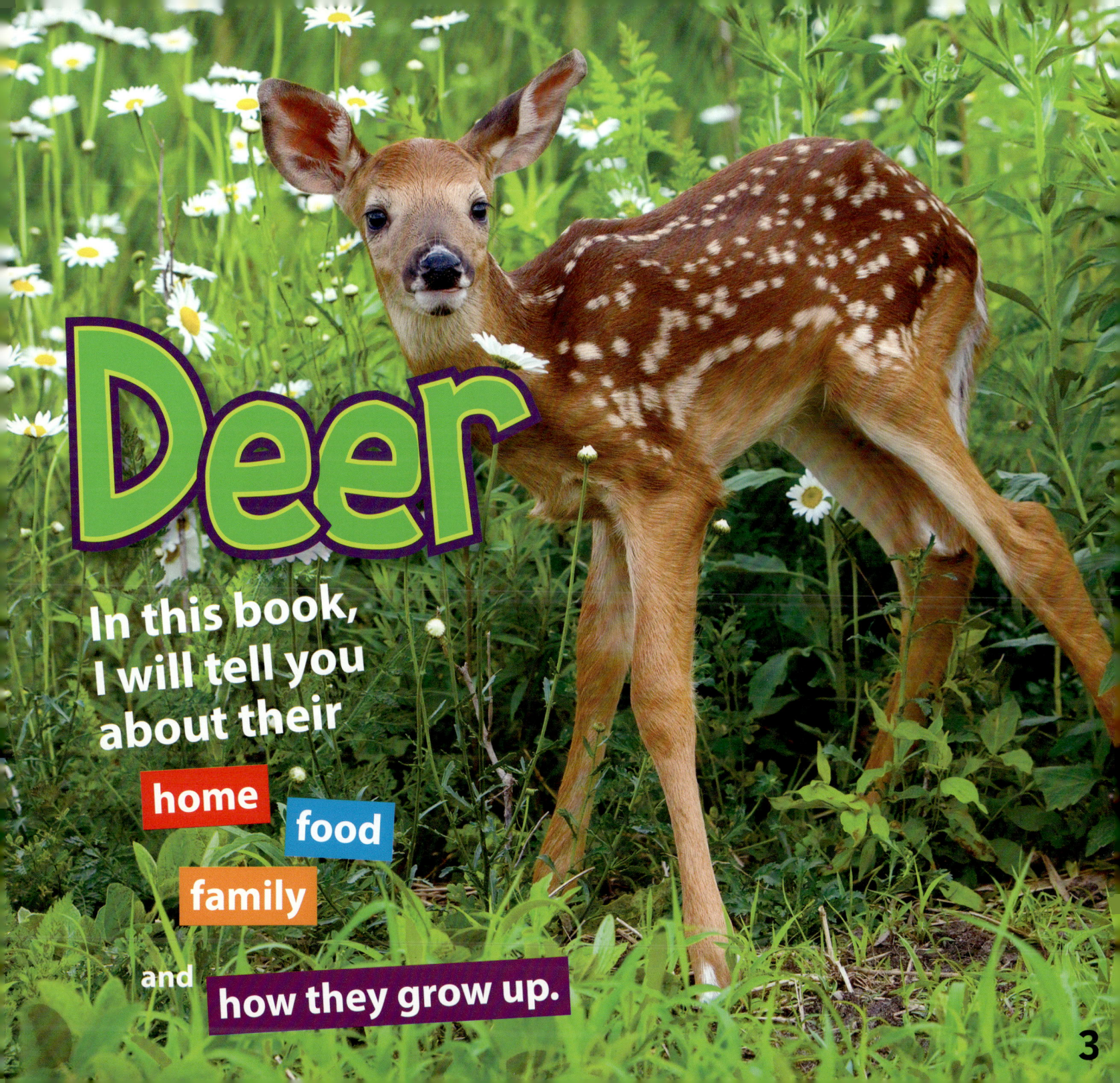

In this book, I will tell you about their **home** **food** **family** and **how they grow up.**

One day, I was walking through the field behind my house. I saw a baby deer lying down in the grass.

I looked around, but I did not see its mother anywhere. I was worried that the baby was all alone.

5

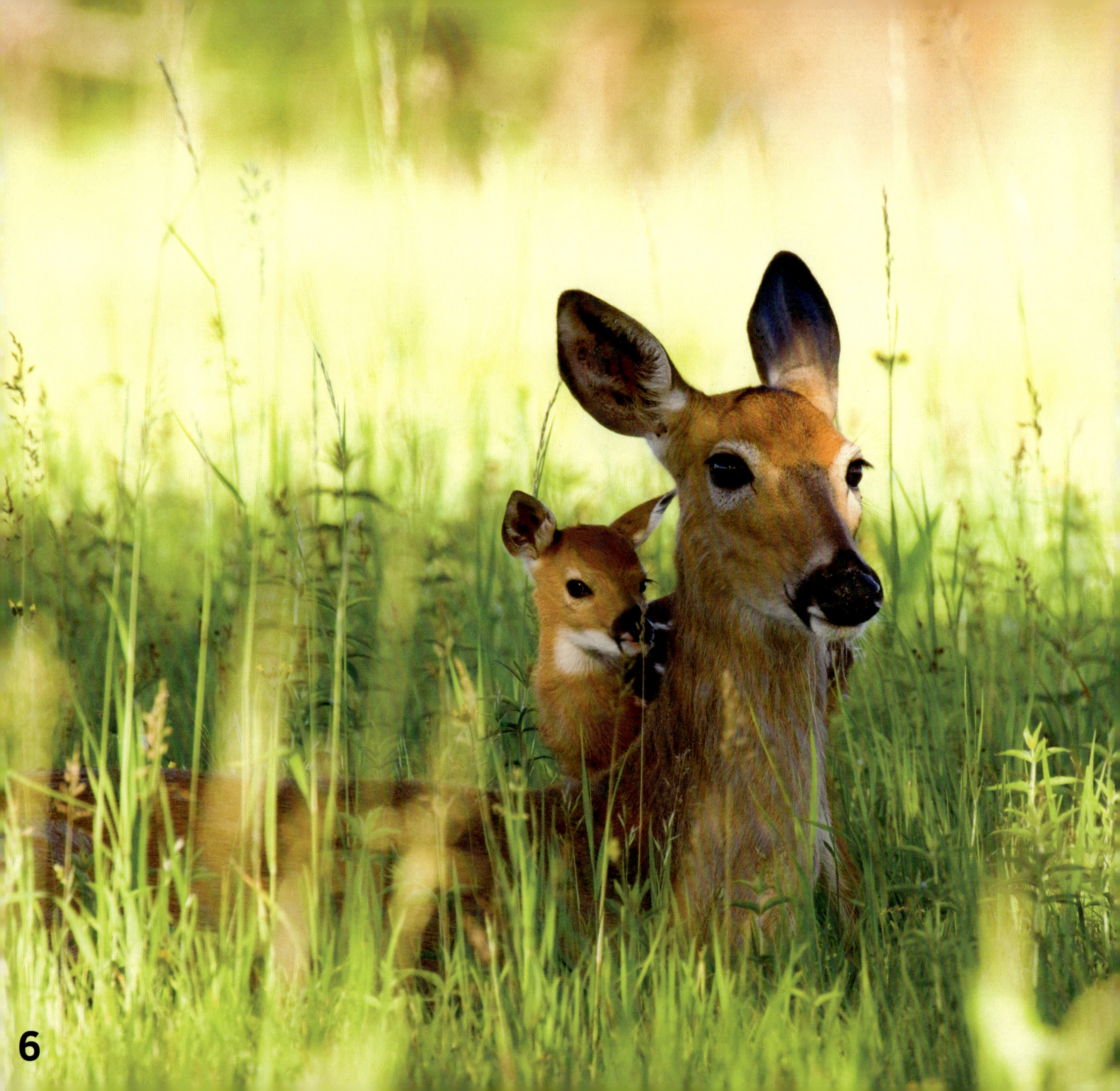

When I got home, I told my dad about the baby deer. He said that mother deer hide their babies in the grass.

My dad said that I should never touch a baby deer. He said the smell on my hands might bring other animals to the deer. These animals could hurt it.

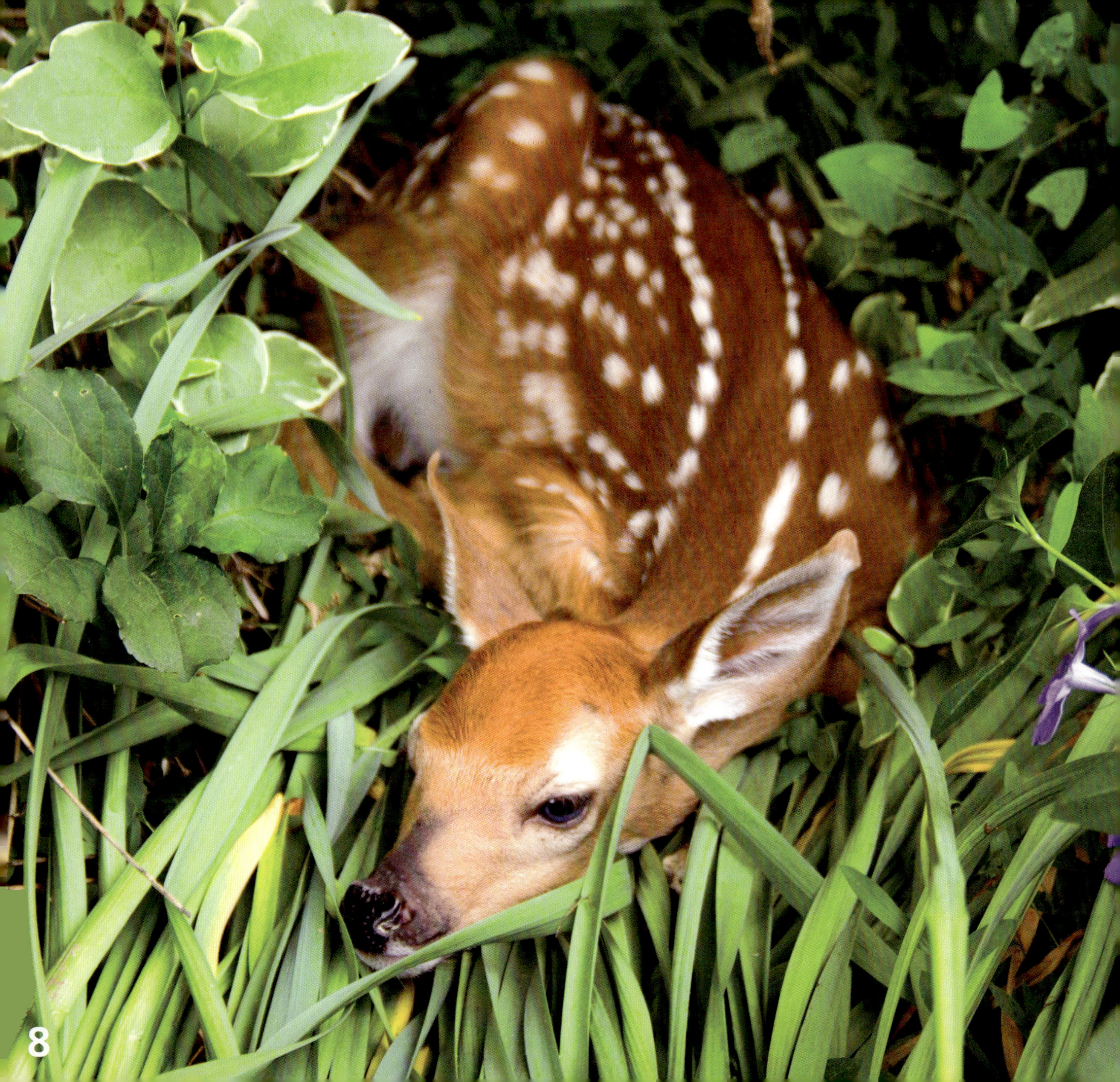

I checked the field the next day. It took me a while to find the baby. The mother deer had hidden it in a new place.

The baby had brown fur with white spots. Its legs were very long and skinny.

I went to the far end of the field to watch the baby. After a while, the mother deer came back. I sat very still so that she could feel safe.

I watched her take care of the baby deer. She fed her baby milk and cleaned its fur.

11

12

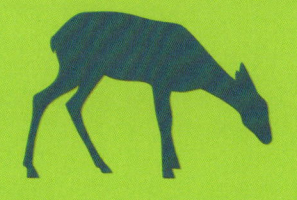

It was not long before I saw the baby walking with its mother. The baby looked bigger, but still had its white spots.

It followed its mother very closely.

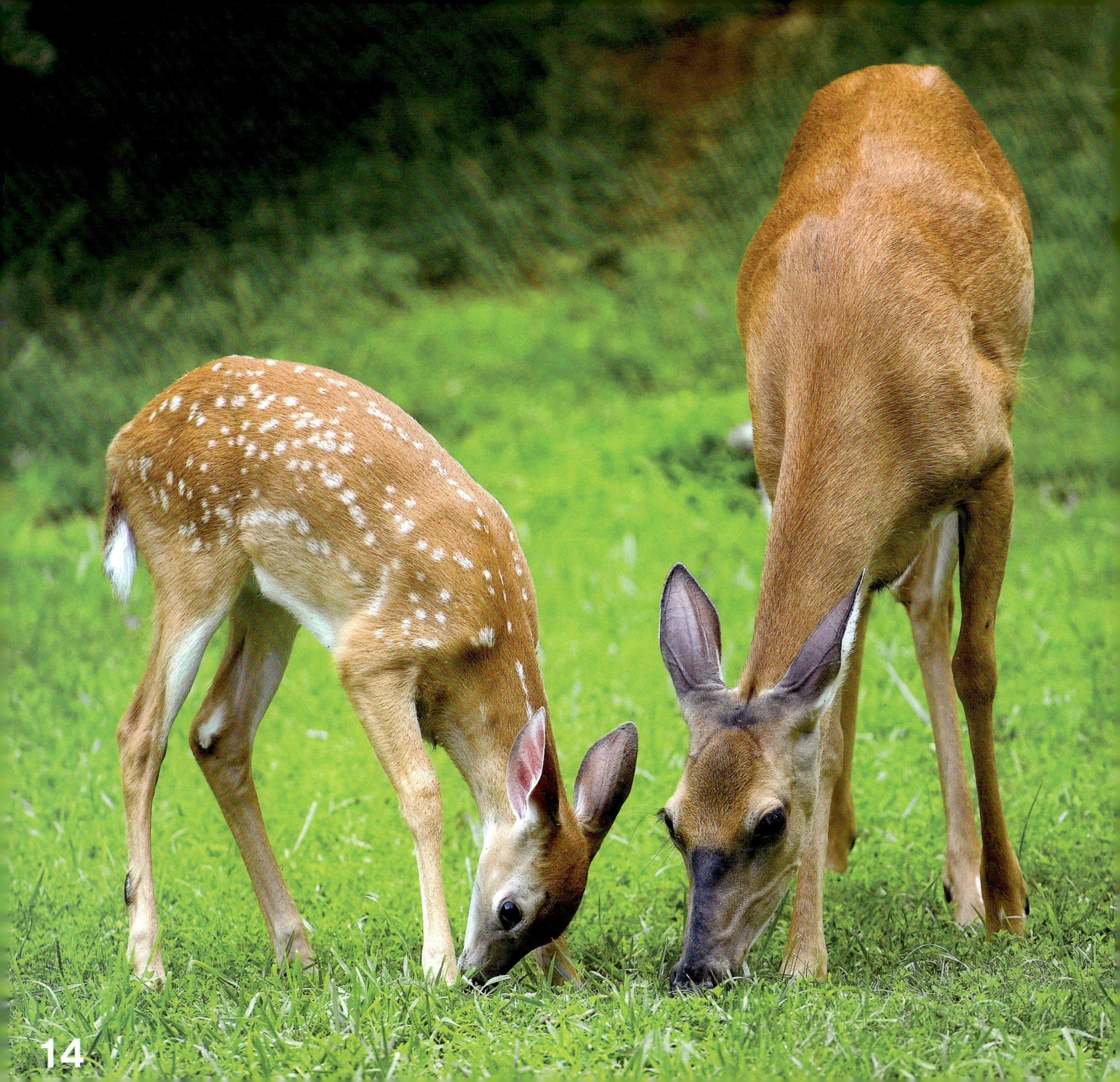

The baby deer was now eating the same food as its mother. They walked through the field eating grass and other plants.

Sometimes, the baby would still drink its mother's milk.

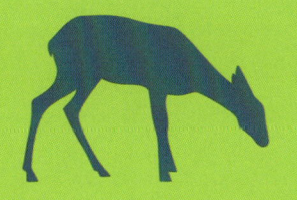

By the end of the summer, the baby deer had lost its spots. It looked like a small adult deer.

The mother and baby both looked bigger than they had when summer started. My dad said they were eating more to get ready for winter.

17

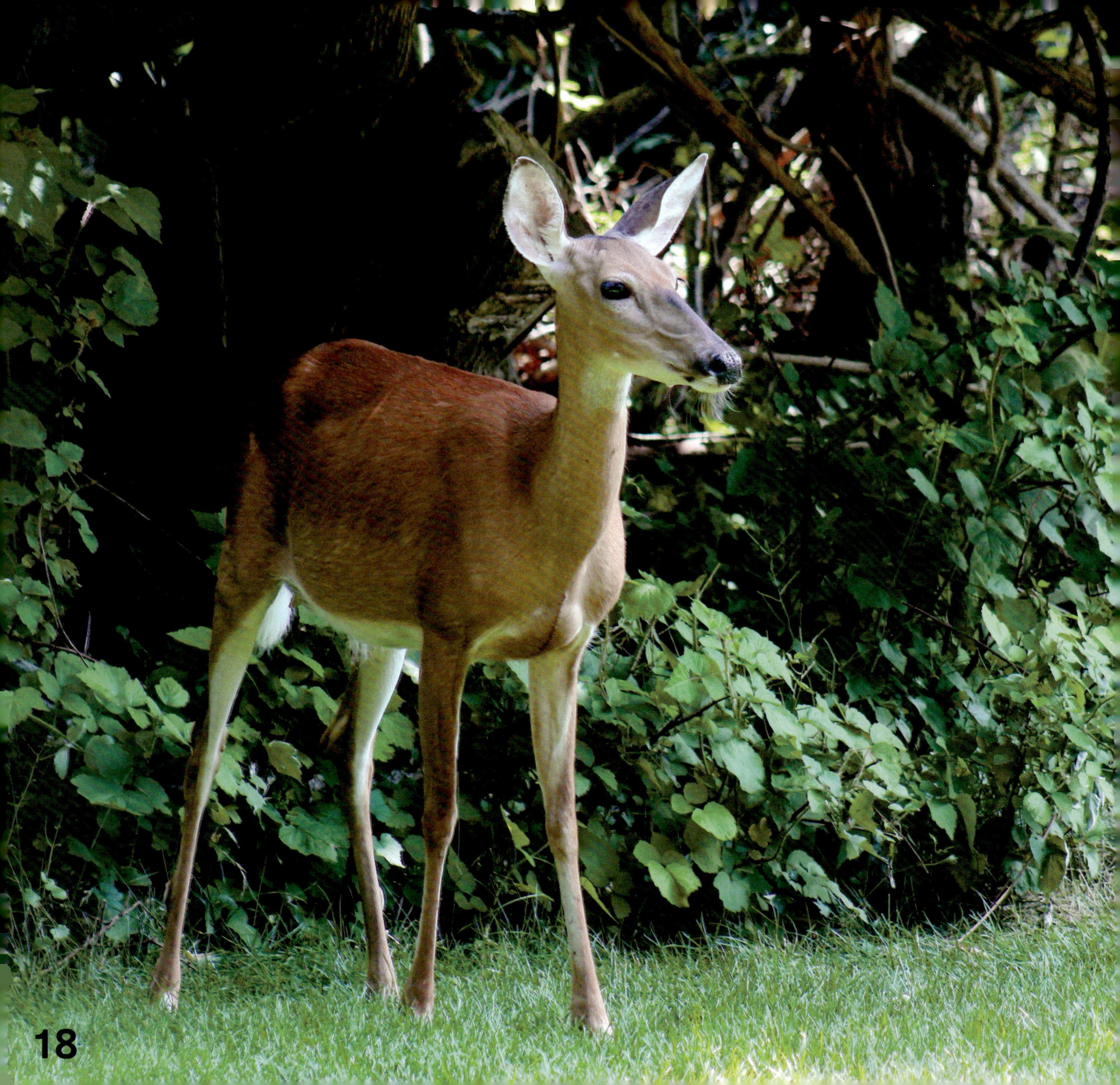

It was time for me to go back to school. One day, I looked in the field when I got home.

I saw the mother deer, but I could not see her baby.

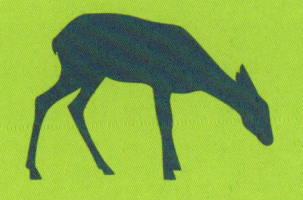

It started to get colder, but I still liked to go outside to play. Sometimes, I saw groups of deer together by the trees.

Some of the deer had horns that looked like branches. In the winter, I found some of these horns in the snow.

21

The next spring, I was walking in the field with my dad. He pointed across the field to a deer.

It had horns like little spikes. My dad said that he was one year old.

KEY WORDS

Research has shown that as much as 65 percent of all written material published in English is made up of 300 words. These 300 words cannot be taught using pictures or learned by sounding them out. They must be recognized by sight. This book contains 97 common sight words to help young readers improve their reading fluency and comprehension. This book also teaches young readers several important content words, such as proper nouns. These words are paired with pictures to aid in learning and improve understanding.

Page	Sight Words First Appearance
4	a, all, around, but, day, did, down, house, I, in, its, mother, my, not, one, saw, see, that, the, through, was
7	about, animals, could, got, hands, he, home, it, might, never, on, other, said, should, their, these, to, when, would
9	and, find, had, long, me, new, next, place, took, very, were, while, white, with
10	after, back, came, end, far, her, of, she, so, still, take, watch, went
13	before
15	as, food, now, plants, same, sometimes, they, walked
16	both, by, for, get, like, more, small, started, than
19	go, school, time
20	found, groups, play, some, together, trees
23	little, old, year

Page	Content Words First Appearance
4	field, deer, grass
7	dad, smell
9	baby, fur, legs, spots
10	milk
16	summer, winter
20	branches, horns, snow
22	spring
23	spikes

Check out www.av2books.com for activities, videos, audio clips, and more!

1) Go to www.av2books.com.
2) Enter book code.   P682462
3) Fuel your imagination online!

www.av2books.com